Whatever Happens to BEAR CUBS?

by Bill Hall

illustrated by Virginia Parsons

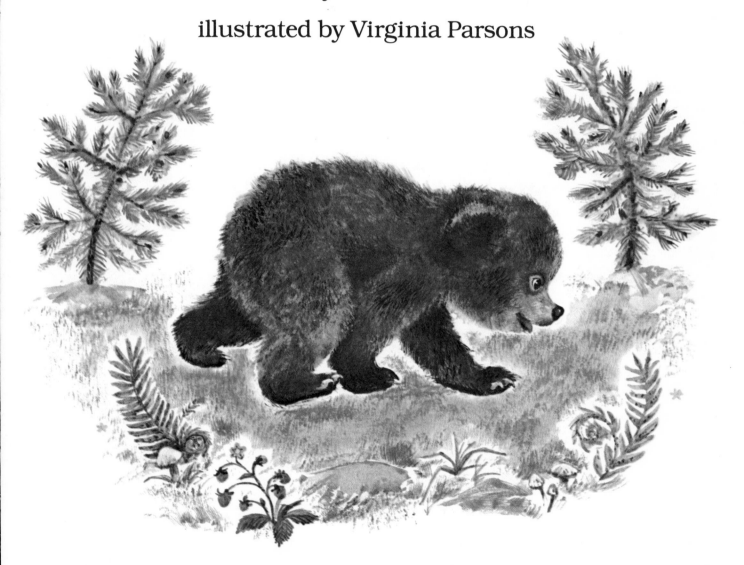

MERRIGOLD PRESS • NEW YORK

NEWBORN bear cubs, no bigger than rabbits.
Bear cubs, who purr when they are babies
and bark when they are big.

Bear cubs are born in secret places—under the snow,
in caves, and in the deep woods.
     Black cubs, white cubs, and brown cubs—
whatever happens to bear cubs?

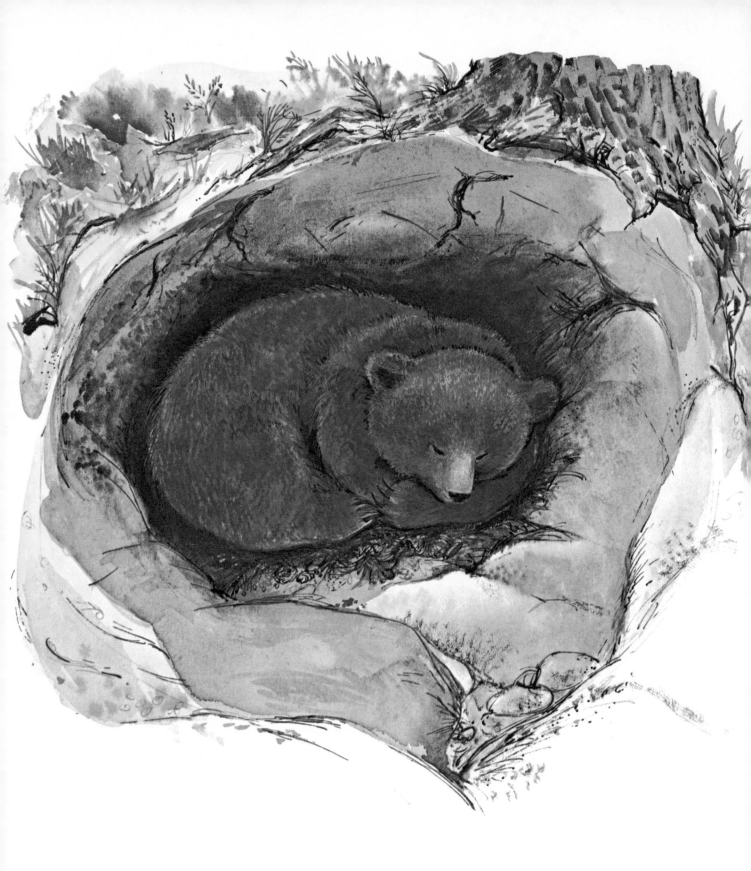

Like a giant furry dog, the mother bear,
fat from berries and fish, lies down in her cave.
She is going to take a winter nap—for three months!

Now the mother has waked up from her long sleep.
And snuggled close to her, she has two cubs—just born,
and hidden in the folds of her fur so that you can't see them.

You can see them now, but they can't see you.
Their eyes are still closed. They have little tails,
big paws, and very sharp claws, the better to hang on
to their mother's thick fur when they are drinking her milk.

Two bear cubs. The mother watches them as they crawl
to her on their bellies, using their front paws to pull
themselves along.

They can see you now. Their eyes are open.
They can hear a little, too. But they can smell things
better than they can see them or hear them.

Soon the two bear cubs are playing like kittens.
They cling to each other and roll over and over together.

They try to jump and they try to box.

Their fur is getting thicker.

They are growing bigger.

Now their legs are stronger. They can walk!
On four legs, and then on only two.
They climb over everything, even their mother,
and they chew on twigs with their new teeth.

The mother has not left the cave to get food for herself
since she started her long nap But where is she now?
The cubs are huddled together—alone in the cave.

Mother is back! Where was she? Maybe she was smelling the spring air to see if it was safe to take her cubs for their first walk. She nudges them out of the cave and into the snow.

The cubs blink in the sunlight and then follow along
in their mother's footprints. They sniff at the snow
and eat some of it and then they start to play.
Their mother plays with them in a very gentle way.

The two little bears are almost grown-up now. They are about to start off together on a hunt for berries and fish.

And that's what happened to these bear cubs
while other cubs were being born to other bear mothers.

Whatever happened to this bear cub?

He can ride a bicycle.

Whatever happened to this bear cub?

He is in the zoo.

Whatever happened to this bear cub?

He has his own spectacles.

Whatever happened to this bear cub?

He learned how to roller-skate.

Whatever happened to this bear cub?

He has a boat of his own.

How do bear cubs get so big when they are born so small?

Like this one—for you.